Learning the Word for Life

BOOK I
FOUNDATIONS

A DEVOTIONAL
DESIGNED TO HELP PEOPLE
MEMORIZE, MEDITATE & INTERNALIZE
THE WORD OF GOD

"PictureThis!" Ministries, Inc. is an evangelical, non-profit 501(c)(3) organization dedicated to serving the Christian community world wide.

Scripture taken from the New King James Version. Copyright 1979, 1980, 1982 by Thomas Nelson, Inc. Used by permission. All rights reserved. Printed in the United States of America.

"Learning the Word for Life!"

A few years ago, a pastor friend shared an interesting observation. He felt that our Great American Society had a severe and life threatening vacuum. "Twenty years ago", he explained, "new converts entered our church community with a sometimes tweaked, but basic understanding of right and wrong." Times and people have changed; the strong Judeo-Christian values which once formed the foundations of our moral and ethical life-style have been undermined. This explains, of course, why the moral fiber of our society is deteriorating, but it should also be a flashing red light for church leaders. With all of our world-wide evangelism and discipleship programs, there still exists today a severe "word-deficiency" in society and, unfortunately, in many of our churches.

A mighty woman of the word, Henerietta Mears, once remarked that, "A teacher has not taught until the student has learned." Information can be brilliantly presented by a teacher, but it does not become "learned" until the student has understood and reformatted this information into his or her own cognitive process. It must become theirs- a part of their thinking and living before it is actually learned. Simply put, the objective of this book is to get people of all ages and cultures **into the word of God so that His word can get into them.** May this book "prime your pump" and in some way, provide a delightful catalyst for a life-long habit of memorizing and meditating on the word of God.

One more important prefacing statement: the Scribes and Pharisees in the New Testament times made a tragic mistake regarding God's word. They were experts in the Law, but basically devoid of spiritual understanding. Consequently, being blinded to the deeper, fuller meaning of the Scriptures, they missed God's greatest blessings. "The Law was given through Moses, but grace and truth came through Jesus Christ" (John 1:17). As great as the Bible is (and it is awesome), it cannot give eternal life. Only the Spirit of the Living Word can do that.

Dan & Juanene Peters

"PictureThis!" Ministries, Inc. Thousand Oaks, California

"Learning the Word for Life!"

❖❖❖ 1 ❖❖❖

A WORD ABOUT GOD'S WORD

GOD SPEAKS... ABOUT HIS WORD

Just as most books contain a Forward or Preface by the author, God has made several comments about His own word. David, whose love for God and His word is expressed so beautifully in the Psalms, is moved by the Holy Spirit to declare, "You have magnified Your word above all Your name" (Psa. 138:2). Later, Jesus will say, "Heaven and earth will pass away, but My words will by no means pass away" (Mark 13:31). Through Isaiah, God emphatically affirms, **"So shall My word be that goes forth from My mouth; It shall not return to Me void, but it shall accomplish what I please, and it shall prosper in the thing for which I sent it"** (Isa. 55:11). Moses brings the priority of the word "down to earth" as he warns Israel, "man shall not live by bread alone; but man lives by every word that proceeds from the mouth of the Lord" (Deut. 8:3). Little wonder that Satan wants the word removed from our currency and county courthouses. However, before we cast a stone at the "heathen," we must as believers, re-examine the priority which we have assigned to God's word in our own lives.

THE WRITTEN WORD

God has spoken, and His word has been recorded by men "as they were moved by the Holy Spirit" (II Pet. 1:21) to give us a faithful and trustworthy record. God's sovereign, guiding hand in watching over the integrity of His word passed down through the ages, is as miraculous as the contents of the Canon (Psa. 12:6). His word is the "document" delivered to inhabitants of this planet to bring us into a living, vital relationship with Himself. It is the "Manufacturer's Manual" designed to show us how to live (and rule) on earth today, and it gives us the keys to eternal life. The word of God is the most powerful "instrument" known to man.

THE LIVING WORD

The Apostle John tells us, "In the beginning was the Word, and the Word was with God, and the Word was God and the Word was made flesh" (John 1:1, 14a). We may well ask, "What is the correlation or connection between the Living Word "(Jesus), the spoken word of God, and the written word of God?" A simple analogy may help.

Imagine yourself standing before a group of people. You identify yourself: "Hello, my name is John Doe." Imagine that the words came out of your mouth, but did not disappear into the world of sound waves, rather they became visible and suspended in space (as it were), right beside you. Then, as everyone watched, your words took on a body of flesh, a mirror image of you, John Doe.

This analogy breaks down of course (as all analogies do at some point), because you are not God. Yet a principle remains: Jesus is the "express image of His (God's) person" (Heb. 1:3). and the written word is an expression in another form, of that same God . That is why, when God's word is planted in a fertile heart of faith, life happens. His word is alive (John 6:63, Heb. 4:12).

THE SPOKEN WORD

God spoke, and the worlds "were framed...so that the things which are seen were not made of things which are visible" (Heb. 11:3). He spoke and a universe came into existence- a cosmos which man's most sophisticated technology cannot measure... not today... not ever... because only God's mind could comprehend it. When God spoke to Abraham, tissues were renewed, blood invaded dried up organs... and a century year old man and woman gave birth to a son. God sent His word to Israel and healed them (Psalms 107:20). When Jesus, the Living Word, walked on this earth, He spoke (as the Father told Him) and the lame walked, the blind could see, lepers were healed. When Jesus spoke, the wind stopped, demons fled, a decaying corpse came back to life. When Jesus spoke, the inherent, creative, mighty power of God's word was unleashed.

Because God is Himself infinite, His word has not and will not lose it's power. As we listen to His word spoken, the vibrations of a supernatural sound wave enter our mind, impact our heart and faith is created (Rom. 10:17). No other stimulation to the human ear drums compares to the tender "massage" of the Master's word, giving hope, encouragement and vision. His word will penetrate the dulled, drunken mind of an alcoholic, the scrambled brain of the drug abuser, even the comatose patient drifting in limbo on the threshold of death. When

God's word is united with faith in a believer's heart, the "Promised Land" becomes a reality (Heb. 4:2).

Jesus often used simple parables to illustrate profound truths. In Mark 4:14-20, the Master presents what we might call the,"Parable of Parables" in which He compares the seed, sower and soil to God's word, evangelists and spiritual hearts. The process, physically and spiritually, remains a mystery, but His challenge is clear: "If you don't understand this parable, you will flunk My art class" (Mark 4:13, 20).

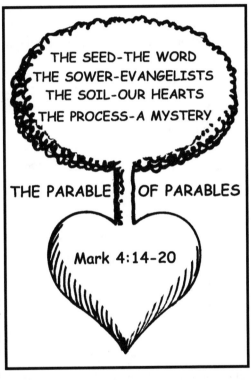

THE SEED-THE WORD
THE SOWER-EVANGELISTS
THE SOIL-OUR HEARTS
THE PROCESS-A MYSTERY

THE PARABLE OF PARABLES

Mark 4:14-20

God promises us that His word will not return to Him until it accomplishes that which pleases Him (Isa. 55:11). Pastors, evangelists and Sunday school teachers are like farmers who plant crops year after year. They have no idea how God's design works, they just know it works- every time. God's word spoken by a loving mother or Sunday school teacher sometimes "hangs around" for years before the light goes on and a wayward child comes home.

THE INTERNALIZED WORD

As we have seen, God speaks and things happen; worlds are created and the course of history is changed. When His word is spoken, a strange "substance" called "faith" is created in a person's spirit. Awesome! However, equally astounding is the transforming, regenerating power of His word when it is embraced by the mind and heart, when it is **"implanted"** (James 1:21) or **internalized.**

Webster's Dictionary defines internalize, "to give a subjective character to, to incorporate (as values or patterns of culture) with the self as conscious or subconscious guiding principles through learning or socialization." This suggests that in the internalizing process, a body of information (or the word of God) first becomes a part of the "self" and then becomes a guiding principle. Once it is "digested" by our conscious or subconscious, it is no longer a separate entity, it is part of the woof and warp of our being.

This is why King David could say, "Your word I have hidden in my heart, that I might not sin against You" and "Your word is a lamp to my feet and a light to my path (Psa. 119:11, 105). Because Your word "lines the walls of my heart", David would say, "I can see the pot-holes and promises in life." The psalmist also declares, "I will meditate on Your precepts...I will delight myself in Your statues; I will not forget Your word" (vv15,16). Here David encourages hiding (putting it deep into our hearts), meditating (chewing on it constantly) and memorizing ("I will not forget") the word of God. While daily Scripture reading is important, a serious student must go beyond that.

The Apostle Paul expresses memorizing and meditation a different way. He exhorted the church in Colosse, "Let the word of Christ dwell in you richly in all wisdom, teaching and admonishing one another in psalms and hymns and spiritual songs, singing with grace in your hearts to the Lord" (Col. 3:16). By whatever means, using all of our God-given faculties, gifts and abilities, let the word of God take root, be at home, reside in our hearts richly. The indwelling word will make us prosperous and productive in everything we do (Psa. 1:3). The riches of His word will make us rich.

Perhaps no other Scripture examplifies the internalizing process better than the incarnation (Luke 1:26-38). Gabriel, having been sent to a young Jewish girl living in Nazareth, announces God's intentions:

she, Mary, will conceive none other than the "Son of the Highest." The miracle, however, was not consummated until Mary **internalized** the word of God by saying, "be it done unto me according to Your word." From that moment, new life began.

THE COMMON DENOMINATOR

The correlation between the written word, the Living Word, the spoken word and the internalized word is expressed succinctly in Hebrews 4:12: *"For the word of God is living and powerful, and sharper than any two-edged sword, piercing even to the division of soul and spirit, and of joints and marrow, and is a discerner of the thoughts and intents of the heart."*

The word of God is living: it continues to create faith (Rom. 10:17) and life (John 6:63). His word is powerful; when combined with faith, it will move mountains and redirect ship-wrecked lives. It is a sharp sword, cutting down arguments of our enemy (Eph. 6:17), and a precise scalpel in the hand of God, revealing hidden motives and secret sins (II Sam.12:9).

❖❖❖ 2 ❖❖❖

THE RIGHT BRAIN / LEFT BRAIN MYTH

HOMO-SAPIENS... MULTI-SENSORY BEINGS

As multi-sensory beings, there are many ways in which each of us absorb new information. One of the most common methods is suggested by the Apostle Paul in Colossians 3:16, *"Let the word of Christ dwell in you richly in all wisdom, teaching and admonishing one another in psalms and hymns and spiritual songs, singing with grace in your hearts to the Lord."* How many of us learned the Bible books

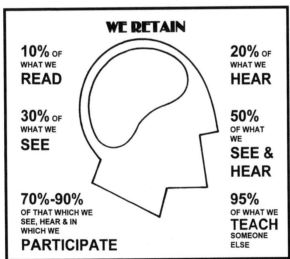

WE RETAIN

10% OF WHAT WE **READ**

20% OF WHAT WE **HEAR**

30% OF WHAT WE **SEE**

50% OF WHAT WE **SEE & HEAR**

70%-90% OF THAT WHICH WE SEE, HEAR & IN WHICH WE **PARTICIPATE**

95% OF WHAT WE **TEACH** SOMEONE ELSE

by singing a simple tune with our Sunday school teacher? David sang the Scriptures and we learn his Psalms today by putting them to music.

One of the most effective techniques used everyday in classrooms around the world is picturing (See Diagram Above). The saying, "One picture is worth a thousand words" is true, and we can be assured... God has given **all** of us this amazing capacity and capability to "picture" concepts. Most people "picture" an act before they do it.

Pictures were around long before written languages. As a matter of fact, pictures were the first language... but a language most people stopped learning in the 2nd grade. (That is why many adults still draw 8 year-old stick figures).

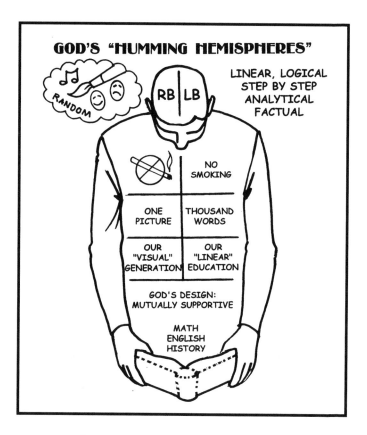

HUMMING HEMISPHERES

Ever wonder why God gave us a 2-sided brain? And why are some people labeled "left-brained" and others "right-brained"? Without attempting to either dissect the human brain or evaluate various internal or external influences, let us say that God, in His infinite wisdom, gave us two cranial hemispheres for a good reason. (See Diagram Above).

First, look at the distinct functions of each compartment. In the right hemisphere, God has equipped us to visualize, imagine, paint beautiful works of art, compose songs and poetry, dream dreams and see vivid visions. Someone has speculated that picturing may be the language of the Holy Spirit.

In stark contrast, the left brain is very logical, linear and analytical. It tends to examine, organize and arrange step-by-step. Much of the external input in our academic world comes to us this way: pages of text, lecture notes, outlines and essays without number. Often messages from our pulpits are devoid of visual aids.

Brain functions, of course, are not mutually exclusive. Just as God has given us two hands to grasp objects, He has given us two cerebral "appendages" with which to comprehend new information. While it is true that some people have right or left brain tendencies, it is also true that everyone constantly computes simultaneously in both sides of the brain. Math involves geometric designs, sentence structure can be better understood by diagraming, science information is often divided into complex tables, and so on. The unfortunate fact is that the right brain potential in the learning process has often been grossly neglected.

LET'S HEAR IT FOR THE RIGHT BRAIN

Times (and signs) are changing. From the Department of Transportation highway directions to General Motors' automobile signage, we are now bombarded with symbols. A restaurant today may post a sign that says, "No Smoking" or one which simply pictures a cigarette with slash through it. Both communicate a message, but pictures, we have discovered, are much faster and more effective. Our brains are highly adept at remembering visual information. International youth speaker Winky Pratney has described this generation as "the most visually sophisticated society in the history of the world."

No wonder our Creator has communicated and continues to communicate with us through pictures. The Scriptures are filled with pictures from which we learn about Him and His expectations. From Isaiah's "I saw the Lord sitting on a throne" to the Prodigal Son, to John's revelation on the isle of Patmos, God paints vivid pictures which enlighten our minds and thrill our hearts. His word is packed with poetry, parables, stories, metaphors, analogies, and other image-building, thought-provoking phrases that trigger our imagination and create pictures.

We cannot help but wonder if the sign of our times (our drift toward a highly visual environment) is connected with God's "Last Days" signs: "...it shall come to pass afterward that I will pour out My Spirit on all flesh; your sons and your daughters shall prophesy, your old men shall dream dreams, your young men shall see visions" (Joel 2:28). Visionaries lead the way.

"Learning the Word for Life!"

❖❖❖ 3 ❖❖❖

MEMORIZING, MEDITATING & INTERNALIZING

PUTTING IT ALL TOGETHER

God wants us to internalize His word. It is obvious that we will miss the deeper riches of His word and a vital power source for our lives if we do not incorporate the Scriptures into the recesses of our heart. How do we do that? Memorize and meditate.

Meditation involves many of the same mental processes as memorizing. When memorizing, for instance, we focus intensely on each word and each phrase, often repeating the words in our mind (left brain activity) or out loud, over and over. We access the right brain hemisphere to build mental pictures and associations. We look for unique sentence structure, repeated words and special emphasis. If we really want the Scripture to "stick", we will say it every day for at least a week and, by the time you have finished this book, we hope you will say it with symbols. If, in the process of the above, we ask God for a "Spirit of wisdom and revelation" (Eph. 1:17), we are on the way to internalizing God's word.

EASING THE BRAIN PAIN OF MEMORIZING

Memorizing is difficult for most of us. It is labor... it brings pain to our brain. Not only do we experience resistance from the enemy in this area, many of us feel that we do not have the cerebral capacity or capability to hold information (even the word of God) in our brain very long. We read, listen, even try to remember, but as one evangelist said, "Our brains have a bad leak!" How can we make the Bible stick in our minds and hearts with the least amount of pain?

WELCOME TO SYMBOL CITY!

As we mentioned earlier, symbols and words have equal power to communicate, but symbols are faster, more effective and FUN! Educational therapists sometimes refer to symbols as "Graphic Organizers." The "PT Power Symbols" illustrated below specifically designed to help you internalize the word of God. By using symbols to draw Bible concepts, you are deliberately activating and applying your right brain power in the memorizing process. Then, as you continue to associate that graphic symbol with the word concept, you will discover that an image is being imprinted on your mind (giving you amazing retention) and being implanted on your heart, which by God's miraculous design will change your life. Again, the process of seed, soil and fruit remains a mystery, but it works.

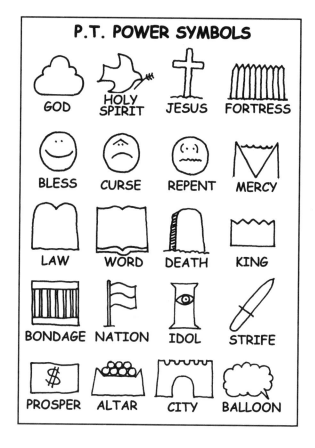

The remainder of this book contains practical applications of concepts presented thus far. It is designed to help you memorize, meditate and internalize the word of God (and have fun while you are doing it). The following 26 lessons will encourage you to implant at least one Scripture each week for the next six months. Each lesson is divided into 4 parts:

1. **The Symbol Drawing** is an illustration composed of simple lines and shapes to help you (visually) "walk through" the selected Scripture. As you practice, this "flash card" visual aid will quickly burn an image on your brain.

2. **The Progressive Thumbnail** provides a sequence for drawing each symbol while you are associating phrases from the Bible verse.

3. **The Dotted-Line Template** removes all intimidation for non-artists and shows you how to position as well as draw various elements of the illustration.

4. **The Dialogue** page. Once you have memorized, meditated and implanted God's word, complete this page.

The Process: Make several copies of the Dotted-Line Template for practice. Study the selected Scripture. Then, using the thumbnail drawing as a guide, begin to sketch each segment of the illustration on the Dotted-Line Template as you repeat the related section of the Bible verse. Once you have done this several times, start saying the Scripture looking only at the Symbol Drawing (without the words). Close your eyes. You should be able to "see" the drawing and recite the verse.

Learning the Word for Life

BOOK I FOUNDATIONS

MEMORY VERSES

.

GOD'S EVERLASTING COVENANT

Genesis 12:2-3

I will make you a great nation; I will bless you

and make your name great; and you shall be a blessing.

I will bless those who bless you, and I will curse him who curses you;

and in you all the families of the earth shall be blessed.

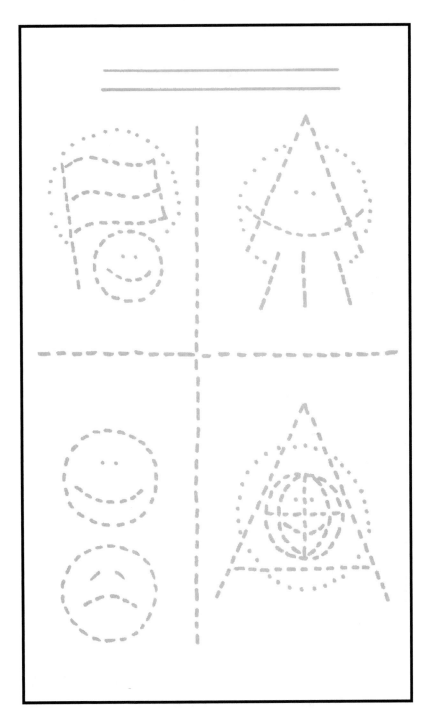

Dialogue with God

GOD'S UNCHANGING CHARACTER

Exodus 34:6-7

EXODUS 34:6,7

And the Lord passed before him and proclaimed,

EXODUS 34:6,7

The Lord, the Lord God, merciful and gracious, longsuffering, and abounding in goodness and truth,

EXODUS 34:6,7

keeping mercy for thousands, forgiving iniquity and transgression and sin, by no means clearing the guilty,

EXODUS 34:6,7

visiting the iniquity of the fathers upon the children and the children's children to the third and the fourth generation."

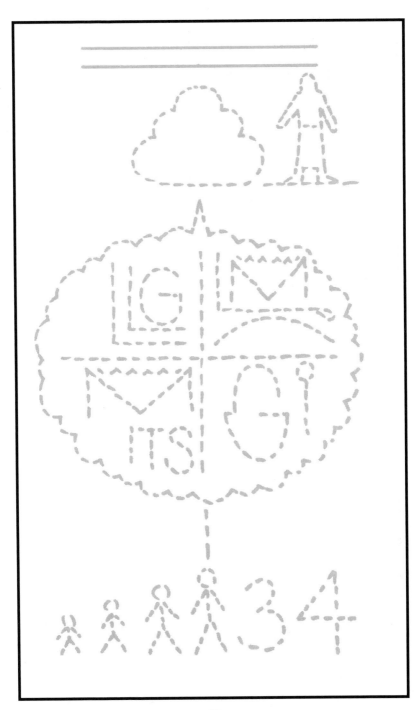

Dialogue with God

By those who come near Me

I must be regarded as holy;

and before all the people

I must be glorified.

31

Dialogue with God

The Lord bless you and keep you;

the Lord make His face shine
upon you, and be gracious to you;

the Lord lift up His countenance
upon you,

and give you peace.

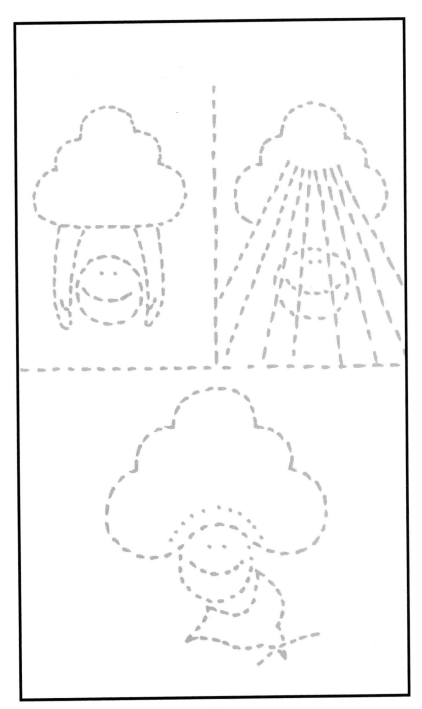

Dialogue with God

WILDERNESS - A NECESSITY

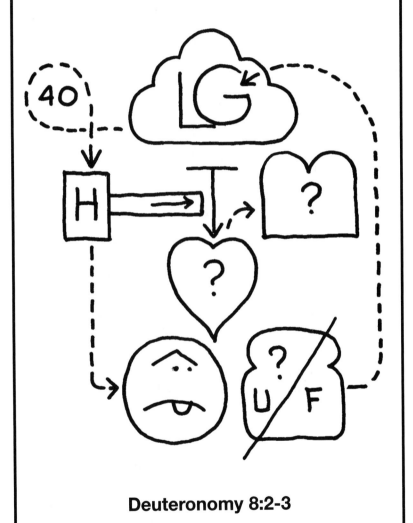

Deuteronomy 8:2-3

And you shall remember that the Lord your God led you all the way these forty years in the wilderness,

to humble you and test you, to know what was in your heart, whether you would keep His commandments or not.

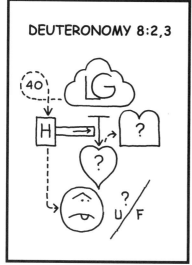

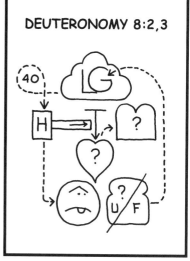

So He humbled you, allowed you to hunger, and fed you with manna which you did not know

nor did your fathers know, that He might make you know that man shall not live by bread alone: but man lives by every word that proceeds from the mouth of the Lord.

Dialogue with God

Choose for yourselves this day whom you will serve,

whether the gods which your fathers served that were on the other side of the River, or the gods of the Amorites, in whose land you dwell.

But as for me and my house,

we will serve the Lord.

Dialogue with God

The Lord repay your work,

and a full reward be given you

by the Lord God of Israel,

under whose wings you have come for refuge.

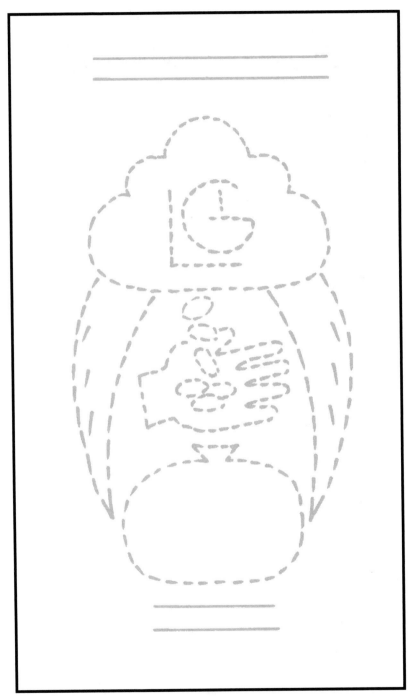

Dialogue with God

PRACTICAL WARNINGS
I Samuel 15:22-23

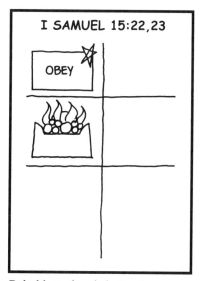

Behold, to obey is better than sacrifice,

and to heed than the fat of rams.

For rebellion is as the sin of witchcraft,

and stubbornness is as iniquity and idolatry.

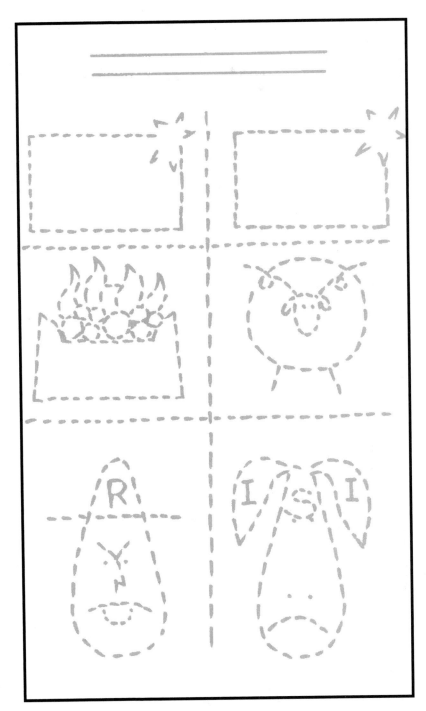

Dialogue with God

RIGHT RULERS

MEN

II Samuel 23:3,4

He who rules over men must be just,

ruling in the fear of God.

And he shall be like the light of the morning when the sun rises, a morning without clouds,

like the tender grass springing out of the earth, by clear shining after rain.

Dialogue with God

Thus says the Lord: "Because the Syrians have said,

'The Lord is God of the hills, but He is not God of the valleys,'

therefore I will deliver all this great multitude into your hand,

and you shall know that I am the Lord."

Dialogue with God

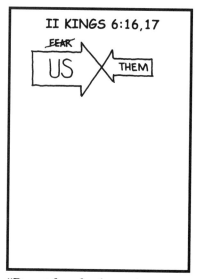

"Do not fear, for those who are with us are more than those who are with them."

And Elisha prayed, and said, "Lord, I pray, open his eyes that he may see."

Then the Lord opened the eyes of the young man, and he saw.

And behold, the mountains was full of horses and chariots of fire all around Elisha.

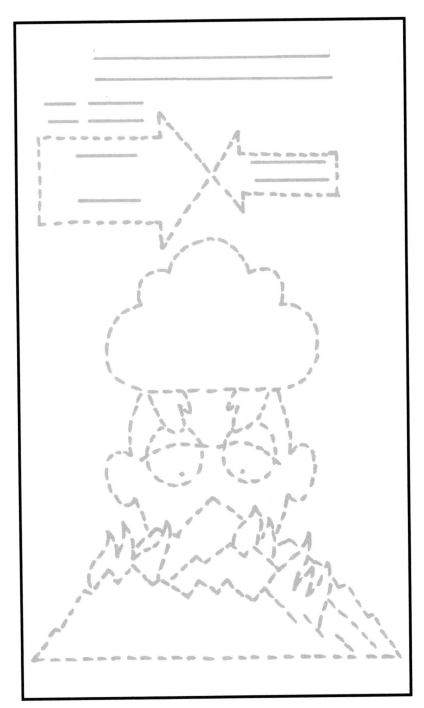

Dialogue with God

ASK BIG!

I Chronicles 4:10

And Jabez called on the God of Israel saying,

"Oh, that You would bless me indeed, and enlarge my territory,

that Your hand would be with me, and that You would keep me from evil, that I may not cause pain!"

So God granted him what he requested.

Dialogue with God

GOD'S PROMISE TO OUR LAND

HEAR

HIS

FORGIVE

HEAL

II Chronicles 7:14

"If My people who are called by My name will humble themselves,

and pray and seek My face, and turn from their wicked ways,

them I will hear from heaven,

and will forgive their sin and heal their land."

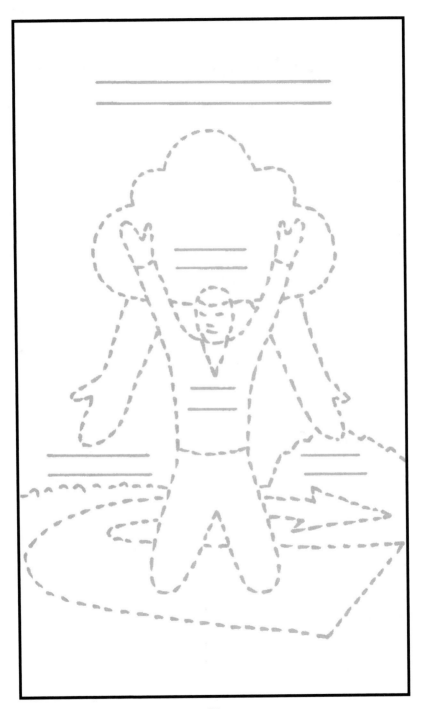

Dialogue with God

For Ezra had prepared his heart

to seek the Law of the Lord,

and to do it

and to teach statutes and ordinances in Israel.

Dialogue with God

GOD'S JOY — OUR STRENGTH
Nehemiah 8:10

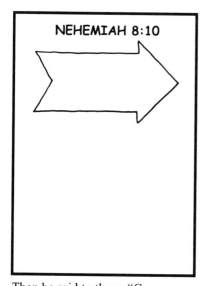

Then he said to them, "Go your way,

eat the fat, drink the sweet, and send portions to those for whom nothing is prepared;

for this day is holy to our Lord.

Do not sorrow, for the joy of the Lord is your strength."

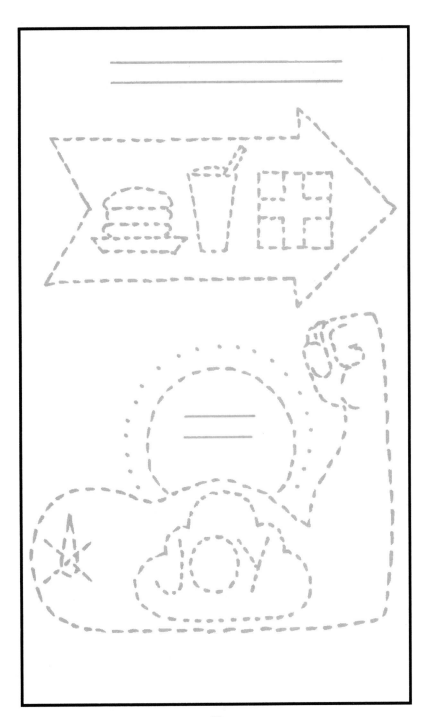

Dialogue with God

BLESSED IS THE MAN...
PSALM 1:1-5

Blessed is the man who walks not in the counsel of the ungodly, nor stands in the path of sinners, nor sits in the seat of the scornful;

but his delight is in the law of the Lord, and His law he meditates day and night.

He shall be like a tree planted by the rivers of water, that brings forth its fruit in its season,

whose leaf also shall not wither; and whatever he does shall prosper.

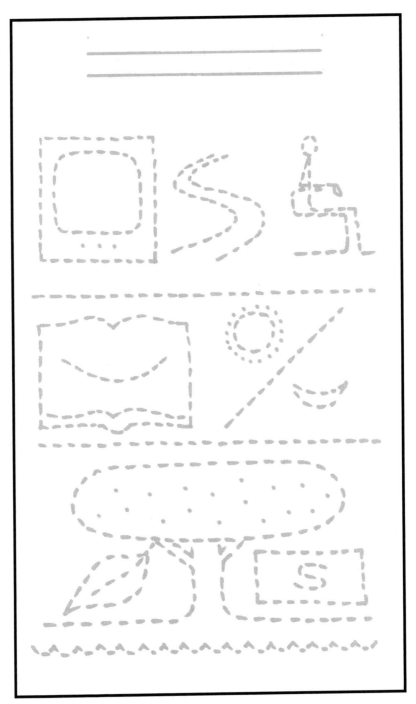

Dialogue with God

GOD'S CARE

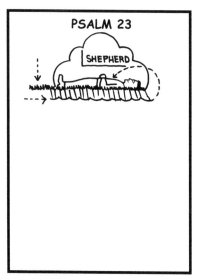

The Lord is my shepherd; I shall not want. He makes me to lie down in green pastures; He leads me beside the still waters. He restores my soul;

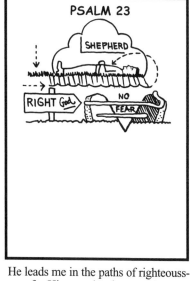

He leads me in the paths of righteousness for His name's sake. Yea, though I walk through the valley of the shadow of death, I will fear no evil; for Your rod and Your staff, they comfort me.

You prepare a table before me in the presence of my enemies; You anoint my head with oil; my cup runs over.

Surely goodness and mercy shall follow me all the days of my life; and I will dwell in the house of the Lord forever.

Dialogue with God

THE COST OF OUR SALVATION
Isaiah 53:1-7

Who has believed our report? And to whom has the arm of the Lord been revealed? For He shall grow up before Him as a tender plant, and as root out of dry ground. He has no form or comeliness; and when we see Him, there is no beauty that we should desire Him.

He is despised and rejected by men, a Man of sorrows and acquainted with grief. And we hid, as it were, our faces from Him; He was despised, and we did not esteem Him. Surely He has borne our griefs and carried our sorrows; Yet we esteemed Him stricken, smitten by God, and afflicted.

But He was wounded for our transgressions, He was bruised for our iniquities; the chastisement for our peace was upon Him, and by His stripes we are healed.

All we like sheep have gone astray; we have turned, every one, to his own way; and the Lord has laid on Him the iniquity of us all. He was oppressed and He was afflicted, yet He opened not His mouth; He was lead as a lamb to the slaughter, and as a sheep before its shearers is silent, so He opened not His mouth.

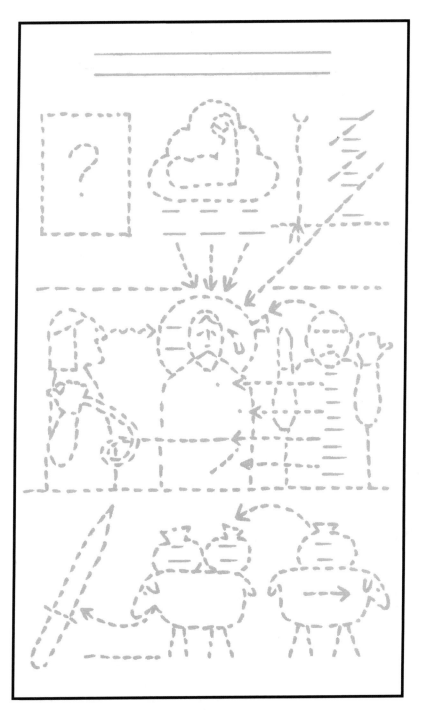

Dialogue with God

GOD'S POWERFUL WORD
Isaiah 55:10:11

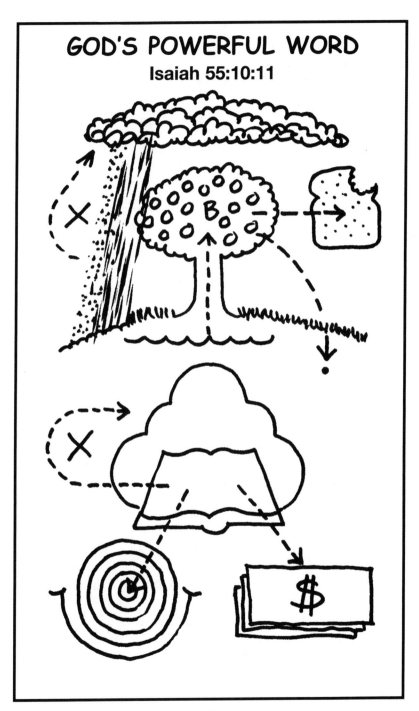

For as the rain comes down, and snow from heaven, and do not return there, but water the earth,

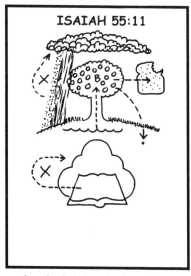

and make it bring forth and bud, that it may give seed to the sower and bread to the eater,

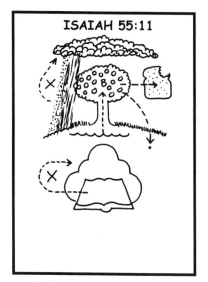

so shall my word be that goes forth from My mouth; it shall not return to Me void,

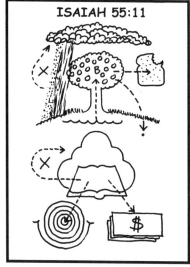

but it shall accomplish what I please, and it shall prosper in the thing for which I sent it.

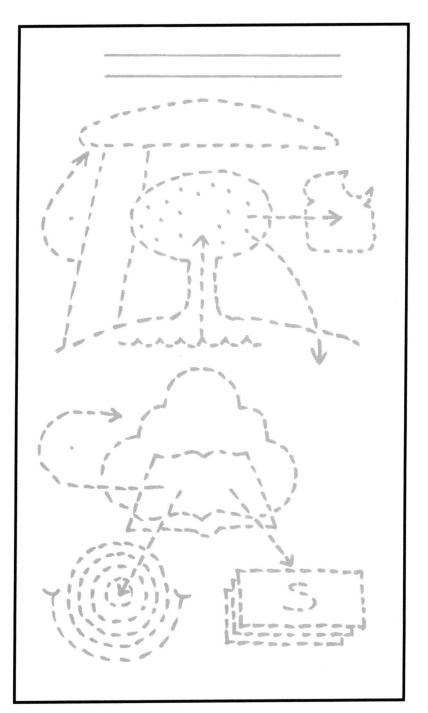

Dialogue with God

THE MINORS

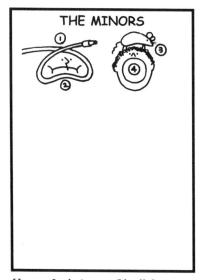

Hosea, Joel, Amos, Obadiah,

Jonah, Micah, Nahum, Habakkuk,

Zephaniah, Haggai,

Zechariah, Malachi.

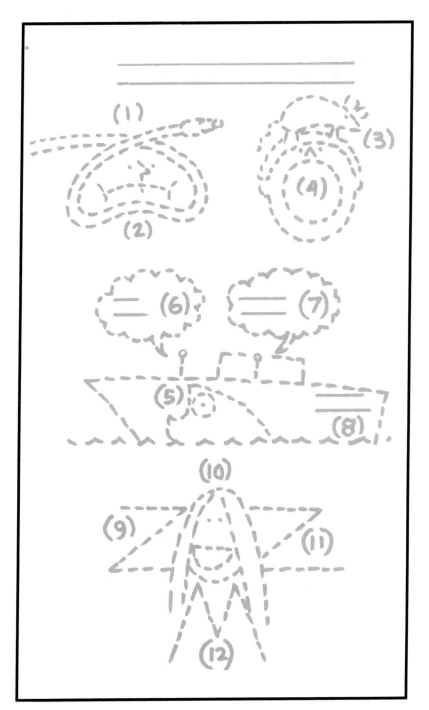

Dialogue with God

FRUIT OF THE SPIRIT
GALATIANS 5:22-23

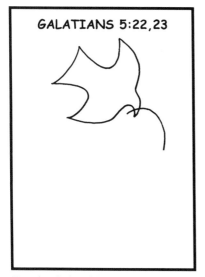

But the fruit of the Spirit is

love, joy, peace, longsuffering,

kindness, goodness, faithfulness, gentleness, self-control.

Against such there is no law.

Dialogue with God

AWESOME WORD

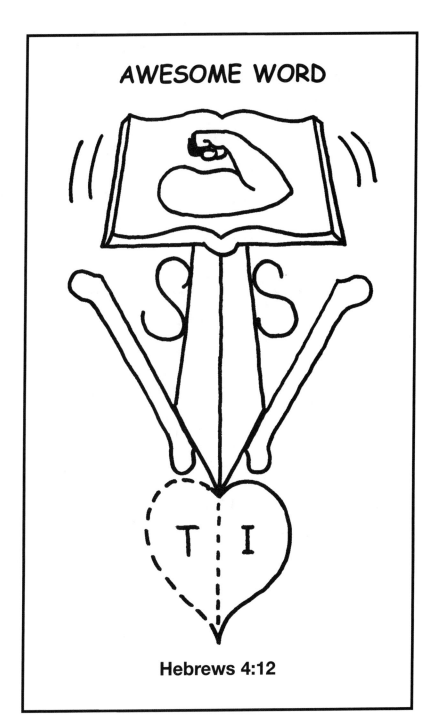

Hebrews 4:12

For the word of God is living and powerful,

and sharper than any two-edged sword, piercing even to the division of soul and spirit,

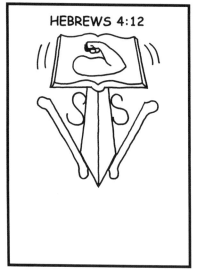

and of joints and marrow,

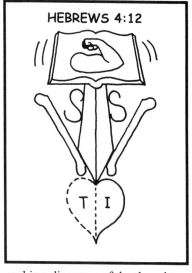

and is a discerner of the thoughts and intents of the heart.

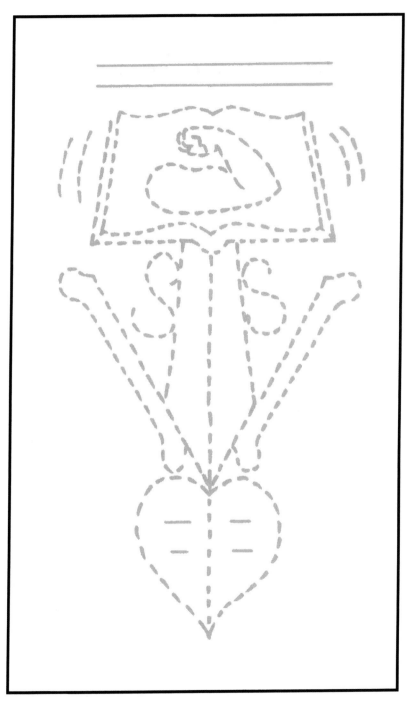

Dialogue with God

LIFE ON MOUNT ZION

Hebrews 12:22-24

You have come to Mount Zion and to the city of the living God,

the heavenly Jerusalem, to an innumerable company of angels, to the general assembly

and church of the firstborn who are registered in heaven, to God the Judge of all, to the spirits of just men made perfect,

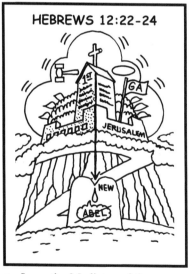

to Jesus the Mediator of the new covenant, and to the blood of sprinkling that speaks better things than that of Abel.

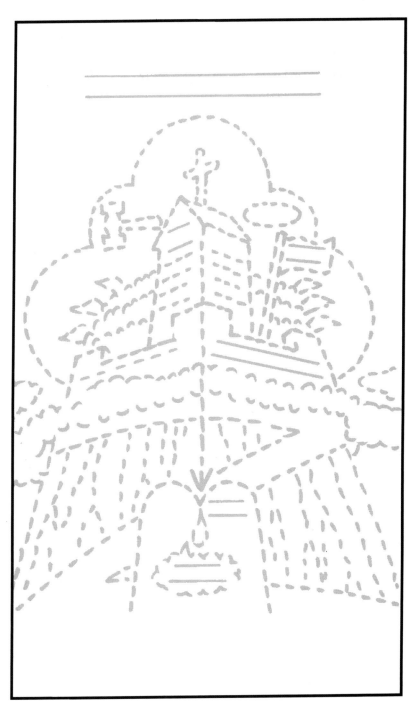

Dialogue with God

He who would love life and see good days, let him refrain his tongue from evil, and his lips from speaking guile;

let him turn away from evil and do good; let him seek peace and pursue it.

For the eyes of the Lord are on the righteous,

and his ears are open to their prayers; but the face of the Lord is against those who do evil.

Dialogue with God

DIVINE POWER

II PETER 1:3,4

As His divine power has given to us all things that pertain to life and godliness,

through the knowledge of Him who called us by glory and virtue,

by which have been given to us exceedingly great and precious promises, that through these you may be partakers of the divine nature,

having escaped the corruption that is in the world through lust.

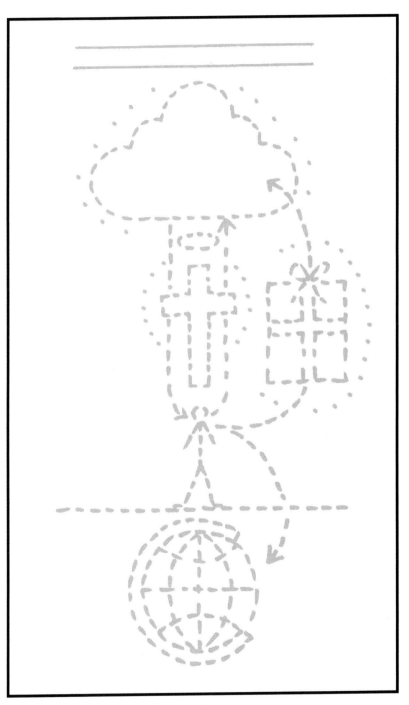

Dialogue with God

Now to Him who is able to keep you from stumbling,

and to present you faultless before the presence of His glory with exceeding joy,

to God our Savior, Who alone is wise,

be glory and majesty, dominion and power, both now and forever. Amen.

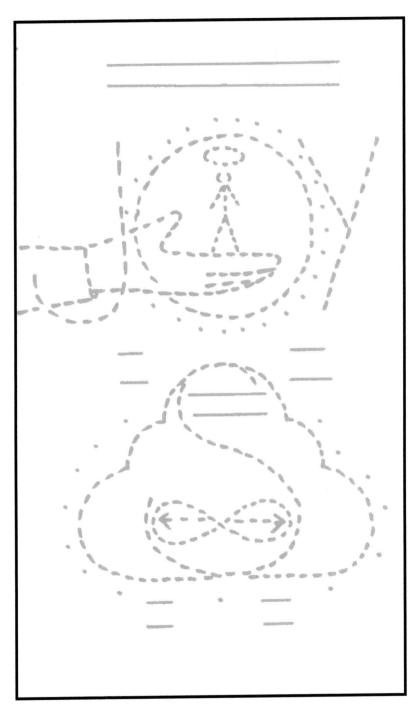

Dialogue with God

Notes

Notes

Draw YOUR WAY THROUGH THE BIBLE!

★ EASY TO FOLLOW DOTTED-LINE ART
★ STEP BY STEP TEACHER LESSONS
★ REPRODUCIBLE STUDENT SHEETS
★ FULL YEAR PROGRAM

Each Bible book (Genesis through Revelation) is illustrated on one page. The teacher follows preprinted dotted-lines while discussing the book. Students listen, watch, & draw the same image, which maximizes retention.

Ideal for:

- Sunday School Classes
- Home Bible Studies
- Christian Day Schools
- Home Schools
- Mission Programs
- Self Studies

"PictureThis!" is available in a 2-Volume paperback set or CD Rom (Mac or PC)

DOWNLOAD A LESSON : www.bibledraw.com
CALL TOLL FREE: (888) 499-9305
OR WRITE: PictureThis! Ministries
236 Castilian Ave
Thousand Oaks, CA 91320

LEARNING THE WORD FOR LIFE!

Life Changers!

Help your friends build a lifestyle
of memorizing, meditating
& implanting the word of God.

GOD'S WORD WORKS!

CALL (888)499-9305 TO RECIEVE
MORE INFORMATION ABOUT:
★ QUANTITY DISCOUNTS
★ OTHER "PictureThis!" PRODUCTS
★ BECOMING A "PictureThis!" DISTRIBUTOR